Angel Anna Siby

I am Angel Anna Siby, a higher secondary student at Al Ameer English School. Never did I fathom that I would embark on the enchanting journey of poetry, yet here I stand as the poet of this cherished collection. I wholeheartedly believe this magic is woven from the blessings of the Lord and the unwavering support of my family, especially my beloved parents. My heartfelt gratitude extends to the esteemed leaders of my school, including respected Principal Jacob Sir, Vice Principal Nowshad Sir and Academic Coordinator Latha Ma'am and our English HOD Ancy Ma'am, whose encouragement has been a guiding light. I am equally thankful to my dedicated teachers, especially Murali Sir, the true architect behind this book's publication, along with Lekshmi Ma'am, Vidhya Ma'am, and Anjukum Ma'am and my class teacher Anupama Mam, who have all played great roles in this adventure. My friends, the A4 Legendary squad, have been my steadfast companions, uplifting me throughout this journey and inspiring me to see it through. Lastly, a special mention goes to my dear friend Aaliyah, whose spark ignited the creation of the poems "Drowning Souls" and "The Lake of the Living."

English Language
From Dust to Life
(Poems)
by
Angel Anna Siby

♦

Published in November 2024
by Kairali Books Private Limited
Thalikkavu Road, Kannur.
Ph : 0497-2761200
E-Mail : kairalibooksknr@gmail.com

♦

Cover Design
Aromal O. P.

♦

76/24-25/Sl.No.1643/100/NS.18.6
ISBN 978-93-5973-044-8

From Dust to Life

Angel Anna Siby

Kairali Books

"Life is a journey meant to be enjoyed, encompassing both joy and sorrow. However, during challenging times, remember not to consider ending it all, as you don't truly possess what you believe you have. Going against this truth will come with a price."

Messages

Dear Angel

We are beaming with pride as you step into the realm of poetry. May your pen be as mighty as sword   and may this milestone mark the beginning of your incredible journey. Your poems have a remarkable way of stirring deep emotions. Let your words touch every soul and spark imagination. Earnestly wishing you immense success and critical acclaim.

Dr. S J Jacob
Al Ameer Principal

Dear Angel

Warmest congratulations on your remarkable achievement as a debut poet. Your work is a testament to your creativity and perseverance. Your unique voice will undoubtedly resonate with readers.
Best wishes for your literary journey.

Noushad Shamsuddeen
Al Ameer Vice Principal

It's heartening to see you explore your passions in a creative way. This accomplishment showcases your dedication and talent.We look forward to witness your future success and the positive impact your writing will have on our community.

Mrs. Latha Warrier
Al Ameer Academic Co Ordinator

Congratulations on publishing your book! It's a huge accomplishment to bring your ideas and creativity to life through writing. It takes dedication, hard work, and passion to complete such a project, and you've done it. Your work has the potential to inspire, educate, and entertain the readers. Publishing a book is a dream many have, but few accomplish. You should be immensely proud of this remarkable achievement.

Mrs. Ancy Dileep
Al Ameer English Department HOD

I am thrilled to see your writing skills blossom. Keep weaving words in to magic. May your words bloom like flowers, touching many hearts and souls.

Mrs. Lekshmi Harikumar
Al Ameer English Teacher

PREFACE

The effort taken by Angel for the completion of her collection of poems is something that cannot be explained through mere words. The poems composed excels by all means especially the thematic presentation and rhythmic words that are exotically enthralling to all the versifiers. The composed poems are enriched with the essentialities of normal human life that transforms personalities from mere dust to elongated real life experiences. This in fact would instill the thought of provocation to transit oneself to a mode of gloriosity from ashes. I personally would suggest to have a vivid reading of each poem which can definitely drive you to a world of reality ironically.

Mrs: Vidhya Sreekumar
Al Ameer English Teacher

CONTENTS

Fairytale

A wonderland is
Where we live in,
A land which has no
Boundaries.

Set with no limits
Wild as it seems,
Is filled with all
kind of creations.
A rollercoaster it is ,
Full of ups and downs

When without limits
It's a fairyland
Indeed, cause none
Oh, I say no one has
Thus found its value yet.
Just as one who has
Set foot into a world
Full of wonders, same
Is the feeling of living
With the purpose
Of unlocking its doors.
One thing I wish,
To speak, do not

Forget to enjoy this
Fairytale, because this is a
priceless treasure forever
♦

Soulmate

Made for each other
May sound easy, but
Everything has its
Own time and value.

Connecting two souls
May sound simple,
Oh, I wish to say
 it's a long journey.

Soulmates are born
When two hearts
decide to adjust their
heartbeats into one.
Through hardships, fights
Sadness and then
Through understanding,
Happiness comes, the
Birth of a soulmate.

Two hearts turned to one,
 a sustainable soulmate
chosen by the heart of
the creator of all creations.

With this they have

Come to a start of
A new chapter the
 beginning of a new life.
◆

The Flame Within

A flame within the
Heart can never be
put out, but only be
hidden deep within.

Though colors express
Its nature and its power,
Each fragment makes it
stronger than you think.

The flame which is carried
deep in you Expresses yourself,
speaking with its power
through your words.
Though you try to hide
it in the darkness, the flame
which is burning is far superior
than you think.

Bursting forth from
The darkness to the
 light of life with all its
 strength at once.

By your side as a

Hidden source of energy
Defending you from
Every evil, giving the ray of hope
From the darkness.

◆

The Anointing

Oh Lord
Hear I stand awaiting
For your call in your
time, amidst the darkness.

Protect me oh Lord,
Shield me under your
Wings, in the loving
Mercies and grace.

Oh Lord, How I wish to
 feel Your Presence Coming
 before you, submitting myself
before thee Oh Lord.
 Pour upon me the oil of
 anointing, which was poured
upon the chosen ones of you oh Lord,
wash me in the oil of holiness.

Oh Lord, give me a new
Heart and a new spirit
in which I may see your
divine revelation.

I here wait upon
You O Lord, bowing in your

presence in await for your
Calling upon me oh Lord.
◆

Everlasting Love

Great are your mercies
oh Lord surrounded
by the eternal glory
no eye sees.

In the midst of twenty
four thrones, oh Lord
You sit on the great white
throne watching the entire
universe.

With the power of the
Words spoken from your
Mouth, your works, oh lord
You began an entire universe.

Though we were not
worthy, Oh Lord you washed
us from the sins we committed
by your love.

As a father loves
his child, Oh Lord, you love us
and we know we are here in
liberty because of that love.
◆

Flame of a Phoenix

She was blessed,
By the creator of the universe
To be the start of the
Of the following generations.

From everything we ever
wanted, showering us with
love and blessings, she stands
beside us at all times.

Her strength is like an
Oak which has fixed it roots
Deep into the earth, which at
All times shall never be moved
 Each day she rises
From the ashes, burning From
deep inside, the flame of freedom
which dwells within her.

As an eagle she covers
Her little ones under
Her wings, shielding
And protecting them
At all times.

As a phoenix which never Dies,
her aim which she still Follows she
keeps it close to her heart, waiting for
a new day to rise up again.
♦

Olive tree

With long slender green
and silver leaves you stand,
amidst everyone bearing
prosperity and beauty.

Shining under the very
Bright sunlight and by it
expressing Your beauty in
all its radiance.

As a home you are to
thousands Of Creatures,
with long life being resilient
you reign for eternity.
Enthroned with a
Crown holding the oil
of anointing, you are a
royal possession.

Considered one among
The holiest part in
Nature, you hold sovereignty
And leadership within you.
◆

Key of life

Life is yours to be
For never let others
Take control of your life
except the Almighty.

Advice is really great
For don't let it be something
You be afraid of, for take control.
For examine everything
You hear let it be
Evaluated then shall it be
Applied to your life.

For don't leave your
Life open for anyone
To just enter and leave
As they wish.
For life is not an open
Road, but its someone's
whole soul that is within it.

For lock it with a key,
keep it secured amidst
everything that comes behind
For whatever you aim to

be yours do not rest until
you conquer it within your arms.
◆

Wake up in life

Why do the nations rage?
Why do they pile up anger in
their hearts? may it be anyone
who stand against?

What is that lies in
their heart that makes them
restless, enough to take a life
among them?

Could it be you, me or anyone
What could be the reason
for this?
why is not an answer be found?
Why does it seem to?
overcome is the only
solutions unto all the problems
that come along in life?

Remember for all
is a Lie, myth and a
misunderstanding while a
little change in the direction
 is enough.

Enough is that to find a cure

To the heart, the cure for
 this lies just before their eyes.

It isn't invisible but
Just lies hidden among the
bushes what we call the
Shadows of the dark.

For if there is no light
There lies no shadow
So that for every problem
That you encounter so
By it a solution is made.

Hate, anger and enmity Can
 be cast out like dust from within
your hearts not that shall be by
someone, but only you.
♦

Nature & Its life

Why do people hate
Nature which is full
With greenery everywhere,
The air fresh and divine.

Which drives all
Negativeness away,
Fills it by goodness and
Makes us energetic all the time.

One who does not take
The time to love and
Experience nature,
Isn't worth living a good life.
The almighty has
Gifted us such wonderful
Elements which sustains life.

Here we are the ones
Who care only to destroy it
Not knowing how to embrace
And adore its beauty.
◆

Dust to life

From dust it all started
Which is called life.
God himself made us
In his image.

The air that sustains
Our life is his gift
We, our beauty our
Health talents are all his gift.

No one should take Pride
into the hearts because
what they possess in this world
cause all belongs to the creator
For no one is in the
sail of the sea of life,
each tides are being
controlled, from alpha to omega
by only one, the Creator.

One must live with peace, love
and unity in their hearts,
with complete trust and obedience
one can achieve success.

◆

The Eternal hope

As the sun rises everyday
so does our hope stay,
a lamp which never runs
out and lies deep in our hearts which
takes us throughout all darkness.

No matter how hard the
path be, never give up hope
as the way, truth and the life
lies just before your eyes.

Once look back from
Where you have become,
Look back from where you began
And even then, and now you are
Feeling like you aren't able to
Come out of the ocean.

For do not be afraid
and keep in mind that
there lies an answer before you,
the eternal love which shall heal
all your wounds and save you.

◆

Imagination

As she searches the
Words of her book
Carefully examining
The book with her look.

As she writes the words
Carefully under the shining light
As she imagines the scenes
As if it were really bright.

She imagines creatures
running around while bees
buzz around gathering their food
busily under the quiet breeze.
As the words quickly turns
into images in her mind.
It's something very interesting
and picturing it is very kind.

As all the creations
take Life in style
of the just world, all that
comes on her face is a smile.

◆

Mystical Canvas

With a splash of colors
to make a magical portrait
to picture a legend or a
mystical adventure.

Comes a splash of emotions
Together to enjoy cultures
Of the land or nations
Which unites its people
As a strong rope.

With a passion of unity
Our forefathers have
Created this magic and we
the beads of this long chain.

 All of us are united and
 a creation of one, like
different dewdrops of
a single cloud.
♦

Light of the world

Oh, the world would
be a heap of ash, as a
result of its sin,
but a hope for their
life had come which will be
their most precious gift.

Rejoice oh you people
as the Lord, Jesus king
of the universe, light of
the world has come to you.

For he comes as a
ray of light to pull you
out from the eternal
lake of fire, to give
eternal life to you.

That you may be called
one among who
enters his kingdom
to receive a crown from him.
Rejoice oh you people
be glad for you are saved by his
rays of glory.

For you are one
among his precious sheep
who follows the shepherd
of eternal light.
 ♦

Guardians

Being perfect in every way,
I am grateful always,
For doing everything for me.
Standing beside me with
guidance love and Care
I ever needed in life.

Whenever mistakes
happen from me, both
of you remains silent
and corrects me.

Being with me through
my darkest and toughest
phases of life, you are my
greatest angels.

Always guiding me
With prayers and advices
You lead me in the
right way, the way of truth
and of life.

I here in this time
feels and will always know,

that I am the most blessed
in the world.
♦

The Rushing Waters

Flowing with no ones
concern, a carefree life of
her own, with a mind
no one could predict, she lives
her life to her wish.

All are her family
though sometimes we
kill her inch by inch
for us to survive indeed.

In a way a saying
is being told that
the little dewdrops
are her children.

With no limits she
rises and thunders roar,
if she decides, her one decision
can bring destruction and
an end to this world.

◆

Melodies

Connected by different
notes to awaken the
hidden emotions in us,
holds a secret bond of
unison in all.

As a sweet bird call
her little ones by her
lovely, charming voice
by enchanting her little one.

So is music to our ears,
enough is that to calm the
frightful storm which
occurs in our heart.

Each fragment which is a
single note holds the chance
for a change, a change
which can redefine humanity.

Life is like a plain
canvas with no colors
when life is without music,
as it is the melody that
should be playing within your heart.

When languages can't
bring unity in the whole
world, music unites
the whole world with its magic.
  ◆

I am Enough

When others tell you
that you aren't enough
which starts a phase
of sadness and depression
in life.

When your closed ones
decide to stand against you
in the battlefield of life,
when things become black
all in a sudden shift of time.

There comes a help,
a help you can never
repay in life, which takes control
of your disturbed heart.

Which helps you to
set your ship to sail
against the storms and
hurricanes in life.

That is a feeling of
hope given by someone
within you, not of this world,

but of a world yet to
be reached.
◆

Dew Drops

Once I was with my
mother watching the
beauty of this world.
Still small and young,
had never experienced
the long journey of life.

Then once my mother
said to me, words I quite
didn't understand at that phase
of time "dear it's time for you
to forward for a very long
adventure of life".

I loosened my mothers
grip set forward with the
mindset my mother trained
me in, began my journey
a new start toward foreseeing
a great adventure.

During the start of this
unforgettable journey,
 i met a new friend a green
leaf, but before I could talk
i met a lot more people

In life.

Later, the journey was
Directed into ponds, lakes,
River and seas and oceans
But when I thought my
Life was settled
Suddenly a change unknown
 took place.

But when things settled,
I heard a very familiar
voice, It was my mothers.
Finally in my heart
i said to myself, I am home,
a place with no worries
in life.

◆

A Father's Love

A love which has no
Limits, no borders
Like the flow of
Rushing waters.

As the eagle teaches
Its children to soar up high
So does the father teaches
His children.

Like a tree which gives
Shade with its leaves,
Is a father who covers
His children under his arms.
A warrior is he
Who loves his children,
Cause he battles everything
In life to make the world a
Better place for his children.
◆

A Change

A time fixed by nature
For leaves to take their leave,
Making way for new ones
To emerge.

Time for birds to
Sing their sweet melodies
For the beautiful passengers
That pass by.

A time for a new
 Generation to emerge, a time
 for the preparation of a welcome
 season for many unknown.
When flowers dance,
Trees bear their fruits,
Where the whole land
Arises with a new aura.

With yellow and tints
Of brown all along the way,
The winter dews wait upon
To take charge patiently.

The fragrance that refreshes
the soul, awakening a
time of a new season in them,
enlightening them and bringing
a new spirit of purity in them.
♦

A Mirror to Reflect

Powerful and sharper than
anything which is formed by the
hands of man, piercing even to the
 divisions of the soul and of the spirit.

A discerner of the thoughts
And of the intents of heart,
By which it upholds all things,
All things by the word of his
Power.

From everything that ever has
Existed, exists and everything
That will be, has sustained
Only because of him.

The seed which sprouts
Into a strong tree which bears
The fruits of the spirit is it ,
A start of a something extraordinary.

The words spoken out
Which have the ability
To change the course of time
Accordingly, to the Creator.
A lamp which guides the way
In darkness and leads us to
Destination.

◆

A Season of Joy

A season of hope is what
Has come, a time of joy,
Of happiness which Cannot
 be measured by any means.

Upon with the wait of
The whole year, the time has
Finally arrived for rain to fall
And people to rejoice, to reap
What has been sown.

Where the hopes of many
Are kept on the rain
herself, in bringing the new
Ways of fortune into their hands.

Where one land expresses
Their emotions as one,
With none to stop them
As the coins of gold and
Silver have come upon them.

◆

Queen of Hearts

A flow of emotions is
What goes through,
When she is seen by
Someone beside her.

She changes her look
And personality depending
By whom holds her hands.

The events in which she
Attends are quite
the ones everyone remembers
By guiding the winds of the hearts.

As a musician control
The notes and harmony
Of a sweet melody,
She changes the atmosphere
Around the one who stand
Beside her.

No one can take that
Title forcefully from her
Cause her lovers themselves
Have enthroned her as the queen of hearts.

◆

A Lover's Perspective

In midst of a million stars,
Standing and leading her beloved
Ones with her shining soft beam
Of light.
She holds the gazes of many
The letters which are told to
her by their eyes.

She is not a lover of
One but many, adorned
With beauty and love,
Keeping her lovers waiting
For her to arrive.
The waters spread themselves
For her waiting for a chance
To capture her beauty
Lest she drifts away.

By the soft shadows of
light, as a young woman
leading the way with a
small lamp in her hand,
Luna, you amaze the people
who love you.
♦

Luminary

At the break of dawn
Arises a new day of life
Filled with inspiration and a
Chance, a chance for a new
Change in life.

Listen to the silent call
Which is deep within you,
The call towards a beginning
Which is undefinable with
Shimmering ideas, a chance
To grow into something no
Eyes have seen.

Embrace the fire that burns
Within you, let your heart
Be your guiding light,
With every step and heartbeat
Let courage and passion flow.

With dreams by your side
As wings, break every chain
Rise like a sun in lives of many
Around you, for you hold
The scepter of inspiration.

◆

Shadows of the Dark

In shadows deep, where silence
Is all what you hear,
A dream unfolds, not what is expected
Where is a place for fear to step in
With whispers all around.

Walking alone through a path
Which seems like it has never
Never been walked upon.

No light for guidance,
Trying to listen to my inner self
Still no voices oh what do I hear
Ah a loud bang is all what I hear.

Darkness takes it all
The presence around me is
Covered with silence
I fall down with numbness.

Suddenly gasping for breath
Thoughts flying back,
I being covered with sweat
Remembers all what has happened
Was a nightmare, a dream
I wish not to think about ever again.

◆

Drowning Souls

A mystery unfolded is what
Has been told, a story it might seem
But its no story but life itself.

Out in the background what is
Seen might bring the picture
Of a perfect story, just like a book
Cannot be judged by it's cover
So is life.

Life as in form maybe like
The waters, which provides life
As well as which has taken many,
As life crushes its own dwellers
Into dust from the same sparks
In which they were created.

Fishes are meant to glide
In the deep waters, but now it
Has come of a time where they
Are drowning deep in their
Habitats which is their life source.
A place where one feels
Most safe in their life,
Has become as the most fearsome
Nightmare present in their lives.

Can these beings be saved?
Or are they destined to drown by
The depths of eternity?
The truth resides within, revealing
One cannot escape the tides and
Storms of life alone.
Yet through the magic of understanding
And bonds of unity, they may
Rise and conquer the trials
They face.

◆

The Lake of the Living

Moments beside the lake of
Life matters than anything,
As each moment matters than
the other, may it be times of
joy and shadows of sorrow.

The lake of the living flows
With emotions, that is needed
To sustain life, though sometimes
It may not flow as planned.

By the breeze which calms
The flow which may at
Times be harsh and unpredictable.
When the flow of waters
Begin some may stand together,
Some may break the core.

Though in midst of everything,
The hardcore devotees of the lake,
Stay committed to be wherever
The lake leads them to be.

◆